Earthforms

Peninsulas

by Ellen Sturm Niz

Consultant:
John D. Vitek
Professor of Geology
Oklahoma State University

Capstone
press

Mankato, Minnesota

Bridgestone Books are published by Capstone Press,
151 Good Counsel Drive, P.O. Box 669, Mankato, Minnesota 56002.
www.capstonepress.com

Library of Congress Cataloging-in-Publication Data
Niz, Ellen Sturm.
    Peninsulas / Ellen Sturm Niz.
    p. cm.—(Bridgestone books. Earthforms)
    Summary: "Describes peninsulas, including how they form, plants and animals on peninsulas, how
people and weather change peninsulas, peninsulas in North America, and peninsulas of the
world"—Provided by publisher.
    Includes bibliographical references and index.
    ISBN-13: 978-0-7368-4308-9 (hardcover)
    ISBN-10: 0-7368-4308-6 (hardcover)
    ISBN-13: 978-0-7368-6142-7 (softcover pbk.)
    ISBN-10: 0-7368-6142-4 (softcover pbk.)
    1. Peninsulas—Juvenile literature. I. Title. II. Series.
GB454.P46N59 2006
551.41—dc22   2004030385

Editorial Credits
Becky Viaene, editor; Juliette Peters, set designer; Kate Opseth, book designer; Anne P. McMullen,
    illustrator; Wanda Winch, photo researcher; Scott Thoms, photo editor

Photo Credits
Bruce Coleman Inc./IFA/IFATR, 8
Corbis/Galen Rowell, 12; Neil Rabinowitz, 16; Sergio Pitamitz, 14
Corel, 1
Getty Images Inc./Lonely Planet Images/Christopher Groenhout, cover; National Geographic, 4
Photo Researchers, Inc./Earth Satellite Corporation, 18
Tom Stack & Associates, Inc./Thomas Kitchin, 10

1 2 3 4 5 6 10 09 08 07 06 05

Table of Contents

What Are Peninsulas?

A peninsula is land with water on three sides. The water can be an ocean, a sea, or a lake. Part of a peninsula connects to the **mainland**. The connection can be narrow or wide.

All peninsulas are different. The land on the peninsula of Florida is flat. Canada's Gaspe Peninsula and the peninsula of Italy both have mountains.

◄ In California's Orange County, many houses fill this small peninsula that extends into the Pacific Ocean.

LEGEND

Land

Water

High Water Level

Low Water Level

How Do Peninsulas Form?

Peninsulas form when the **water level** in oceans, seas, and lakes changes. As water levels rise or fall, more or less land can be seen. When water surrounds land on three sides, a peninsula is formed.

Long ago, many peninsulas formed when rocky plates in earth's surface moved. The huge plates connected all the land on earth. Over time, **magma** flowed between the plates and pushed the land apart. Seven continents formed, each with peninsulas.

◄ An island not connected to the mainland during high water levels may be joined when water levels are low.

Plants on Peninsulas

Climate affects which plants can grow on a peninsula. Many types of plants live on peninsulas that have mild climates.

Cardon cactuses live on California's dry Baja Peninsula. When rain falls, long cactus roots soak up water. Pacific Ocean mists add water to Baja Peninsula. These mists help ball moss plants grow in the dry climate.

On the Alaskan Peninsula cold weather lasts nine months. Mosses and shrubs grow during Alaska's short, warm summers.

◄ On California's Baja Peninsula, this cactus survives the hot, dry climate by gathering water with its long roots.

Animals on Peninsulas

Some animals on peninsulas aren't found on the mainland. Florida panthers once lived throughout the southeastern United States. Today, they only live in southern Florida.

Climate affects which animals can live on peninsulas. Camels live on the hot, dry Arabian Peninsula. They can walk for days in this climate without water.

Polar bears live on the north Alaskan **coast**. Thick fur and fat help them live in the cold climate of this peninsula.

◄ Many Florida panthers once roamed the United States. Today, only about 70 are left.

Weather Changes Peninsulas

Stormy weather can make peninsulas smaller. Hurricanes and storms can cause water levels to rise. Crashing waves **erode** and change the shape of peninsulas.

Waves helped form rock shapes on Australia's Tasman Peninsula. As water rose and fell, waves hit the land in different areas. Sea arches and a **blowhole** formed.

Dry weather can make peninsulas larger. During dry spells, water levels drop. Low water levels can uncover more land.

◄ On Tasman Peninsula, years of erosion formed Tasman Arch. Rising water may someday erode the top off.

People Change Peninsulas

People make many changes to peninsulas. They build **ports** on peninsula coasts. Ships carry supplies to the ports. People also build houses and hotels on peninsulas.

In the early 1900s, people made big changes to the Florida peninsula. People wanted to farm on Florida's wet Everglades. They planted melaleuca trees to drain large areas of water. The trees killed Florida's natural plants. Today, people are working to get the Everglades back to its natural state.

◄ Located near Cap Martin Peninsula (background) this port in Menton, France is mainly used for boating.

Peninsulas in North America

Alaska is the largest peninsula in North America. It is more than twice the size of the state of Texas. Alaska covers 571,065 square miles (1,479,052 square kilometers). Much of Alaska is covered with mountains and hills.

Canada's Gaspe Peninsula also has many mountains, but it is much smaller than Alaska. The Gaspe Peninsula stretches across 11,390 square miles (29,500 square kilometers). It is only a little larger than the state of Maryland.

◀ Many snow-capped mountains cover the southeastern part of the Alaskan Peninsula.

ARABIAN PENINSULA

QATAR
PENINSULA

Peninsulas of the World

The Arabian Peninsula is the world's largest peninsula. It is so big, astronauts can see it from space. It holds six countries. They are Saudi Arabia, Yemen, Oman, United Arab Emirates, Qatar, and Kuwait.

Qatar Peninsula is connected to the large Arabian Peninsula. It holds the country of Qatar. The Qatar Peninsula only covers 4,400 square miles (11,396 square kilometers). It is about the size of the state of Hawaii.

◄ A photo taken from space shows the outline of the huge Arabian Peninsula.

AUSTRIA

SWITZERLAND

HUNGARY

SLOVENIA

CROATIA

FRANCE

BOSNIA
and
HERZEGOVINA

SERBIA
and

MONACO

SAN MARINO

MONTENEGRO

ITALY

Corsica
(FRANCE)

Adriatic Sea

VATICAN CITY

★ ROME

ALBANIA

N

W   E

S

SARDINIA

Tyrrhenian Sea

Ionian Sea

LEGEND

★ = Capital

Mediterranean Sea

SICILY

ALGERIA   TUNISIA

Peninsulas on a Map

Peninsulas are easy to find on maps. Just look for a piece of land with water on three sides. Maps show the outline of peninsulas. Maps also show where peninsulas connect to the mainland. Some maps show mountains, lakes, and rivers on peninsulas.

Changes in water level can change the shape of a peninsula. New maps are made to show changes to peninsulas.

◄ This map shows where Italy connects to Europe. Italy looks like a boot extended into the Mediterranean Sea.

Glossary

blowhole (BLOH-hohl)—a cavelike hole formed in a cliff by years of erosion from the ocean

climate (KLYE-mit)—the usual weather in a place

coast (KOHST)—land that is next to an ocean or sea

erode (i-RODE)—to wear away; wind and water erode soil and rock.

magma (MAG-muh)—melted rock found beneath the surface of earth

mainland (MAYN-luhnd)—largest landmass of a country, territory, or continent, as opposed to its islands or peninsulas

port (PORT)—a harbor or place where boats and ships can dock or anchor safely

water level (WAW-tur LEV-uhl)—the height of the water in an ocean, a sea, or a lake

Read More

Nadeau, Isaac. *Peninsulas.* Library of Landforms. New York: PowerKids Press, 2006.

Olson, Nathan. *Italy: A Question and Answer Book.* Fact Finders: Questions and Answers: Countries. Mankato, Minn.: Capstone Press, 2005.

Internet Sites

FactHound offers a safe, fun way to find Internet sites related to this book. All of the sites on FactHound have been researched by our staff.

Here's how:
1. Visit *www.facthound.com*
2. Type in this special code **0736843086** for age-appropriate sites. Or enter a search word related to this book for a more general search.
3. Click on the **Fetch It** button.

FactHound will fetch the best sites for you!

Index